THE SCIENCE OF MANHOOD:
Steps to self-improvement

by
Derik Barnes

Printed in the United States of America

Library of Congress-in-Publication Data
TTXU001881140

The Science of Manhood: Steps to self-improvement/Derik Barnes
ISBN 978-0-9912737-0-6

Editing and Book Formatting by *JetSet Communications & Consulting*
Book Cover Design by *heydee@ideezyn.com*
Photography by *3lindVision Inc.*

The Science of Manhood is presented by
Clear Vision™. On behalf of the organization I sincerely thank you
for your support of this book project.

CEO & President - Derik Barnes

Contents

❧ ✠ ❧

Dedication

This book is dedicated to my loving wife Akisha Barnes and our children AL-Nas, Precious and AL-Nisa. I thank God for their unfathomable honesty and support. Words cannot express how much I love and appreciate them.

In Memory of

Thelma Minor | Irvin S. Johnson Sr.
Archie S. Reynolds

The Science of Manhood

A few words...

"It is a rare occasion that a man can meet with and engage a group of inner city African-American males. But it seems that Mr. Derik Barnes of Clear Vision has such a gift. I had the distinct honor of meeting this gentleman and I do mean GENTLEMAN. His "slow burning" and smooth desire to reach, teach, motivate and enhance the lives of young people is unparalleled. It's not that he can do the job; it's that he WANTS TO! His credentials speak for themselves. He's battle tested and still shining after surviving life's punches. He has managed to come out of the boxing ring of life battered and bruised but not beaten or defeated. His will- for years to come is to lead the charge in making dramatic inroads into the ever complex and ever changing mind of the young African-American male mind. If you are looking for a man of many gifts looking for the precious and few moments to share them, it's Derik Barnes. As you read his writings rest assured that not only will you be touched by his passions but so will those who receive his wisdom. He's a rare bird indeed, who flies high above the fray but who humbles himself to dip his wings and visit the seeking and misguided masses on the ground. His horizons are far away yet reachable because he teaches the path and leads the way. It's been said a thousand times but truly, if we had more Derik Barnes…the WORLD would be a much better place."

Stanley Smith
City of Baltimore Mayor's Office
Westside Youth Opportunity Community Center

"The Science of Manhood is a great starting point for any male looking to gain control of their productive future. This book is an efficient read with an insider's edge. The author is not just a man with book knowledge but someone who has seen and experienced life on the front line. I suggest and encourage all males to read this book and share the information with others."

Rev. Anthony Van Johnson
New David Baptist Church

"The Science of Manhood" is not just a book but a guide with foundational principles of wholesome values and morals for men of all nationalities. It helps this generation and the ones to come, not to repeat a negative history that many sometimes don't want to talk about. The author is a man that I know personally and he has experienced what he has written in this book. We can always learn from another man's upcomings and downfalls so as not to repeat them in our own life. This book will do just that. It is definitely one to have in your library for a reference. Thank you Derik for sharing your experiences in this book."

Pastor Jimmie C. Thompson, Jr., Senior Pastor
Kingdom Deliverance Ministries International
3527 N. Rolling Road, Suite 8
Windsor Mill, MD 21244

"The Science of Manhood" is an important undertaking. The guide makes an unapologetic attempt to rebuild, resurrect and restore to men of any race or religion an essential quality of life. The information Derik shares will benefit a man's family, peers, community and through a broader scope; the world. He has written this book from a very unique perspective. For several years Derik has worked in various professions that have placed him in direct contact, face-to-face with men who saved lives and unfortunately men who have taken lives. He himself has been inspired by men who rebuild lives through faith, spirituality, clean living and love. It is through the first which I have had the benefit of Mr. Barnes acquaintance. I *over* stand and have faith that "The Science of Manhood" will be a bright light in the lives of men whose lives have become dark. Dark with identity crisis, lack of positive role models etc. I feel that Derik is the right *Person* to bring this light into existence. I emphasize the word person because it comes from the Latin root word *"Per"* meaning *"Through"* and *"Son"* from *"Sonar"* meaning sound. Therefore we are *"persons"* because we can speak things into existence.

The Bible tells us that GOD in the presence of darkness spoke first "Let there be light" and there was light. I know "The Science of Manhood" will be that light in many lives. I was present when it was spoken into existence. What you have in your hands or are listening to is the fruit of a brief conversation Mr. Barnes had with a young man. Mr. Barnes like a scientist breaking down a chemical reaction was explaining in easy to over stand language, how a man should conduct himself in various situations that could adversely affect his life if handled incorrectly, hence; "The Science of Manhood". I listened to this uncommon wisdom and begged Derik to help other men by putting his guidance on paper. I only wish "The Science of Manhood" was around when I was growing up."

Lieutenant Norman Hall
Baltimore City Fire Department

"I have known and been friends with Derik Barnes for close to 15 years. When we first met, he was working as a correctional officer at one of the meanest correctional facilities in North America – Maryland State Penitentiary. You normally expect a prison guard to be aggressive and tainted. Yet, what immediately stood out to me was Derik's affable and friendly demeanor. There was a certain gentle way about him. He was a glass-half-full kind of guy who moved with self-confidence. He was humble. In short, Derik was a winner.

When Derik recently informed me that he had written a book which gives young males a detailed, step by step road map to achieving success and manhood, all I can say is that I was excited and curious. I wanted to read what he had to say.

After reading this book, the only word that comes to mind is WOW!! This is a great book. The book isn't long, but Derik gets his message across loud and clear. We have a crisis in North America concerning young men. As a successful African-American man, Derik dispenses advice on how to overcome the many vices and distractions that plague inner city neighborhoods. His advice is frank and contains no "B.S." Any young man, who reads this book, will have a positive instructional resource to help guide them on their journey to real manhood.

I salute Derik for a job well done. After you read this book, do everything you can to get it in the hands of as many young men as possible. Their futures and the future of the younger generations of men depend on it".

Steven H. Heisler, Esq.

"In the spirit of Martin Luther King Jr., Malcolm X, and other civil rights leaders, Derik W. Barnes has picked up the torch in a way that many others have not. I love his passion and actions when it comes to reaching out and assisting with shaping the lives of our youths. Derik's book, "The Science of Manhood: Steps to Self Improvement" addresses many things from a Spiritual, Mental, and Emotional standpoint that most men don't talk about but needs to be said and heard. This is a NEW blueprint for a different generation, where values may have changed, but the problems still exist. "The Science of Manhood: Steps to Self Improvement", should be in every classroom, home, library, or wherever men, especially young men, congregate."

Phinesse Demps
The Baltimore Times & MY SOUL RADIO

The Science of Manhood

Foreword

I would like to thank Brother Derik for giving me this opportunity to say a few words as it relates to manhood. He, like so many of us when we were young came through a process to Manhood, but again it's a process. Bro. Derik points out 24 steps in that process by which he arrived to manhood in hopes to shares these great steps with many of our young brothers who need them as a guide through the difficult maze of life. In the African tradition a young male goes through the rites of passage called "simba". The word "simba" means "young lion" and it is the boy's introduction into manhood. It is then when he is taught the process or science of being a man. What Bro. Derik gives in this book the Science of Manhood is so crucial today as it is so needed for our young black males. 70% of the homes today in the Black community are single parenting homes, which are headed by females. On the other hand 70% of the jails are full of black and hispanic men, so we don't have to ask "what happened to the men?" A child psychologist by the name of Jawanza Kunjufu author of the book "Raising Black Boys" mothers raised their daughters but love their sons" what he's saying is, women cannot make boys men, it takes a man to make a man.

I believe this book Bro. Derik has written will help guide those young males who have no father figures to become men. This is only the tip of the iceberg but it is the beginning process to get these young males to manhood. Bro. Derik and I are products of the teachings of the Hon. Elijah Muhammad who trained us to become men through our F.O.I (Fruit of Islam) training. Every young male must have an example of what a real man looks and acts like. That shining example of manhood for Bro. Derik and I has been and is the Hon. Minister Louis Farrakhan. By way of such an example Bro. Derik has been able work with all races and cultures as a Community leader, Correctional Officer and presently a Firefighter. Each process is a stage which represents a mighty work in progress. Manhood training is so critical today for our young males. Some may ask why; so that we can guarantee a future of strong responsible men who will respect and protect their women, children and the elderly of the community. Men who understand their moral obligation to help establish the kingdom of God right here on earth! It's only through the process of manhood that they can begin this great journey from Boys to Men.

"I Am Present for Peace"

Captain Dennis Muhammad
Founder of the Peace Keepers

Acknowledgements

I would like to thank the Men and Woman of the Baltimore City Fire Department, specifically the firehouse of Squad 54, Truck 30 and Medic 13. There have been many days and nights when we would have "NO LIMIT KITCHEN DISCUSSIONS" on all types of topics. You name it, we talked about it. However, one evening in particular we were all engaged in a deeply heated conversation about how one's manhood is tested in different situations. From that conversation the idea for this very book was born. I want to thank all of my brothers from Squad 54: Lieutenant Norman Hall, Ken "Carlos" Johnson, Francisco Carreras and John Agadja. I would also like to thank my brothers from Truck 30: Lieutenant Tim Davis, Ameer Peace, Kenny May, Robert Huff Jr. and Brian Spina. These men have all made footprints of inspiration within this book. It's an honor to serve the citizens of Baltimore City beside you and I could never thank you enough.

The Science of Manhood

Introduction

Science: A systematic knowledge of the physical or material world gained through observation and experimentation.

Manhood: The state or time of being a man or adult male person; male maturity and traditional manly qualities.

This isn't "feel good" fiction or a drama-filled novel; this is a direct lifeline thrown in a desperate attempt to help revive the rapidly decaying image of young black men, and males in general. I wish I had the time to eloquently describe the bountiful traits displayed within these pages. Unfortunately, time is limited. The death toll for young black males throughout the inner cities is increasing by great numbers. Parents are burying their sons more frequently than ever before. The prisons are bursting at the seams with young men. Our communities are overrun with violence, mostly at the hands of young men. In this book, I strive to reveal some of the steps and strategies to redirect our young men away from a path of riotous living, incarceration, and death.

The Science of Manhood

Step One
Have Faith
❦

"Faith isn't faith until it's all you're holding on to."
— Unknown

I'd love to be able to tell you to keep your head up, think positively, and have a winning attitude and life will work out just fine. But the truth is, it's a dark world out here, and you will be tested far beyond what you're normally used to. A young man can easily find himself weighted down by the pressure of a careless society that seems to grow colder by the day. Such overwhelming opposition must be met with an even greater force, and that force is—that's right—the Creator! Call him whomever you like—be it Jehovah, Allah, Jesus, Yahweh, Jah —just call on him! Try to remember that "faith is the substance of things hoped for," and you must tap into that unfathomable source of strength and wisdom to counteract or withstand the vice-like conditions around you. I can vividly remember times in my life when things seemed to have been turned completely upside down—family issues, career trouble, no transportation—and I couldn't understand why. I had no answers; my trust in people was weakened and things started to really fall apart all around me. In my darkest hour, I called on him for understanding and strength, and the creator delivered. Having a spiritual source can definitely revitalize and rejuvenate, but you must do your part to stay as productive as possible. So many young men cry, "I can't find a job… I'll just give it all to God." No, sir! You can pray and ask the Creator all you want,

21

but you'd better be asking for strength and guidance to fill out some job applications. Let us remember brothers, as the old saying goes, God only help those who help themselves.

Step Two
Mannerism = Mind, Body & Spirit
❧ ✢ ❧

"You can mold a mannerism, but must chisel a character"
— Unknown

In many of the inner cities throughout this nation, the streets are overrun with young men who are lost with no direction. This can be seen in the way they act, their style of dress, and the language they use. Captain Dennis, founder of The Peacemakers, said, "We must teach our youth what is expectable behavior vs. unacceptable behavior as it relates to their conduct in their community." In other words, changes are going to have to be made in order to shine a better light. Just observe the average young man on a daily basis: you'll see slumped posture, head hanging low, pants sagging around his ankles, and aimless wandering. I'm sure this isn't all young men, but in most inner cities, this is what you'll find. In order to achieve recognition as a man, we must exhibit the character of a man: stand up straight, walk like you have somewhere to be, speak up, master a firm handshake and eye contact; these are the marks of true manhood. Most of us have been taught to only dress up for special occasions—church, funerals, and court dates—as if that's the only time worthy of looking your best. Well that isn't the case, nor should it be. As a man, you should strive to look, sound, and smell right and exact (with the exception of employment if that's what your job requires) at all times. Every man seeking to maintain manhood should own a suit. You can achieve this in a mall or thrift shop, and I assure you that people will treat you completely different. I remember as a young boy watching my step-dad dress and the way that his well-groomed attire seemed to almost command attention and respect. Whenever there are important meetings, you'll find most men in business suits, ties, pressed shirts, and shined shoes. As we go about our travels in pursuit of jobs and business opportunities, you want to look your best, because when you look your best, you'll feel your best and that's when you give the best you have to offer. As men, we should invest in quality toiletry items, select a worthy barber, learn how to tie a tie, and select nice shoes. Always remember that steel sharpens steel, so find a good brother or family member who appears to maintain a more refined image and lock in. Another area we should strengthen is our verbal control. Brothers, we must enhance our vocabulary so that we can be understood clearly when communicating with others. One of the problems I had to deal with was profanity. I had a hard time with that until I started to study and increase my vocabulary. We should use our PC for more than the social media, brothers. Look up some of the powerful men who make things happen and study them; read information that makes you want to take the whole world by storm. You must think like a world ruler, and until you think, talk, walk, look, and smell like it—it will never be, dear brother.

Step Three
Feed your mind and body right
~~❦~~

"It's up to you today to start making healthy choices. Not choices that are just healthy for your body, but healthy for your mind." — Steve Maraboli

I could not stress enough how important it is to maintain your mental and physical health while striving to balance your quest for manhood. Now when I speak of feeding yourself right, surely I'm not just talking about lunch and dinner selections, but also what we feed our minds, brothers. Just as a man makes careful choices not to overeat and watches his caloric intake, he should be careful of any negative information he takes in his mind as well. Let's us start with the television, or "TELL-LIE-VISION" when not carefully handled. It's easy to fall into everything and end up with nothing by depositing too much of our time and attention into things that don't add to our progress. Brothers, this also goes for those who spend countless hours on PlayStation and Xbox. While this is fun, relaxing, and entertaining, it is something to enjoy only after key things are in place. Brothers, a man shouldn't be in front of a TV or game system for hours if he hasn't secured a decent level of employment for himself. As men, we should be on top of all the job openings in our grasp. Ask yourself before you sit down to dive headfirst into a game of "Madden" with the guys: Have I done anything to move forward today? How many applications with resumes have I submitted today? Do I even have a resume? Do I have a shirt and tie pressed and ready to go right now? If you answered "no" to these questions than you need to get up and get it done, ASAP! If you're sitting home all day watching reality TV that affects everyone's reality but yours, if you're home all day counting baby daddies on daytime television and singing every song on the radio, word for word while you lack job interview skills, you're slipping. By no means am I judging anyone, and no, I don't have all the answers. Most of you are far smarter than I am; however, I have invested more time into self-improvement than most others have. I remember looking in the newspaper for jobs, and all I would see was "three years' experience required," this is needed, that is needed. I loved playing PlayStation and running ball with the guys at the park, but that wasn't going to help me get anywhere in my job search. I had to change the direction of my attention, and I did so by first getting off the game and hitting the library and bookstore to learn more about the field of employment I wanted. The guys hated that I wasn't running ball, but I had to replace that time

> *Have I done anything to move forward today?*

with job fairs, interviews, training, and studying. All that I'm saying, brother, is that we have to make the most of our time. We only get out what we put in. Now as far as eating your meals, you should be mindful of what you put in your body for the simple reason that you only get one body. The more discipline you muster up, the easier it will be to maintain good health, and this means not eating just anything, at any time. I know, I know, it sounds like

I'm hounding you, but don't you worry, declining health will slow you down soon enough. High blood pressure, diabetes, and strokes do not have to be our reality. Most illnesses are mostly due to the poor eating habits that most of us refuse to give up. As a man, take control of your eating habits as best you can. I know it's hard to get back in shape after we have become out of shape. Many helpful books and programs can help us get back into the fight; so, hang in there and don't give up, brothers, because your body is your temple.

DETERMINATION

PUSH4

Bill Gates: Gates didn't seem like a shoe-in for success after dropping out of Harvard and starting a failed first business with Microsoft co-founder Paul Allen called Traf-O-Data. While this early idea didn't work, Gates' later work did, creating the global empire that is Microsoft.

PROGRESS

Step Four
Enrich your circle
❧ ✤ ❧

"If a man does not make new acquaintances as he advances through life, he will soon find himself alone. A man should keep his friendships in constant repair."
— Samuel Johnson

"Everyone is someone because of someone else." That said, we must understand that the company we keep is of great importance. As young men, if we are striving to obtain the traits of manhood, then we must surround ourselves with like-minded people who are reaching just as high, if not higher, to do the same. You and the people around you should have an agenda—a destination of greatness. Whenever we entertain an environment contrary to the one we are trying to progress in, there's a chance of falling off track, brothers. This happens; no one is perfect; this is a process, and it takes time. By no means am I promoting perfection. Maintaining manhood can be a tedious journey, yet one of the most rewarding journeys, so we must hang on and maintain. Many brothers find strength in the brotherhood found in churches, community recreation centers, young boys' clubs, Mosques, temples, etc. The main thing is to become a part of something greater than yourself so that you can draw strength from it and still add value to it with your presence. I must be honest; I had very little understanding of manhood other than the basics, such as working and paying bills. It wasn't until I encountered the brothers in the F.O.I (Fruit of Islam) that I was shown an active example of manhood. The F.O.I are the men of the Nation of Islam. They specialize in making men with manhood training classes not found anywhere else in the world. The classes helped me to take my life to a new level, and I owe a great deal of credit to the Nation of Islam for my development. Now while the F.O.I was my route to training, it might not be yours, and that's fine; as long as you find what you need somewhere. Let us be found being productive alongside brothers who understand that the role of the men in our community is in dire need of repair. The more of us who submit to the light of manhood training, the greater the chances a young man will find his way out of darkness by our example.

Step Five
Build your library
❧ ✣ ❧

"To add a library to a house is to give that house a soul."
— *Marcus Tullius Cicero*

Take a moment and think about all of the great men who came before us and all the things you admire about them. Maybe it's the courage of Frederick Douglass, the diligence of Dr. Ben Carson, or the heart and ambition of your own father. Whomever you admire for whatever reason, they too studied someone at some point in their lives. As men, we should take the same approach by reading, studying, and researching the lives of men and women who have made honorable contribution to humanity. As young men seeking information to broaden our visions, we must start accumulating a library. There are hundreds of books, lectures, and even audio books available. All young men aren't the same and some of us need more of an up close and personal connection. I made the effort to look up everything that had to do with self-improvement, such as powerful speeches by Les Brown, Anthony Robbins, and Eric Thomas. These are just a few of the outstanding authors and motivational speakers who can help ignite the fire of inspiration burning deep within each of us. We must stay plugged in and updated on current events. We have to know what's going on around us to make the moves we need to make in a timely fashion. Many of us move far too slowly to be effective due to the lack of information. Read your newspapers, and sit down to watch the local and worldwide news. Continue to arm yourself with knowledge so that you can accurately combat the ignorance that surrounds you.

Step Six
Love your brother as you love yourself

"We must live together as brothers or perish together as fools." — Rev. Dr. Martin Luther King, Jr.

I know, brothers, this sounds a little too simple, but unfortunately, the statistics show a far different picture. An analysis of Missouri Police Department statistics shows that black males made up 65 percent of homicide victims in Baltimore, Atlanta & Chicago from 2007 to 2014. It breaks my heart to see this as a reality in many of the cities across America. We must strive to change this harsh reality, and change starts with men caring and loving themselves and the community. I listen to the radio and I love hip-hop as much as, if not more than, most people, but we don't need another song about killing n%@!#, big butt freaks, and popping bottles. I hear all the songs about being cold as ice, smoking on green, and being in the trap. It's painful to see us dancing to the sound of our death and degradation as black men. The way we parade our ignorance before the world shows a lack of true love and self-worth. I feel as though I have the right to feel some kind of way about hip-hop because, along with many others, I have taken time out to take part in the hip-hop summit in which some of these very same artists pledged to do better. Again, I love our hip-hop and R&B artists. I just know if we were to promote more positive music, it could help change our plight. Without a doubt, I must thank the entire body of artists who have used their gifts to uplift and reach our youth. One of hip-hop's biggest icons, Snoop Dog (now "Snoop Lion"), took a stand and drew heavy attention to the problem of negative music in our community. In a recent interview, Snoop acknowledged his negative influence through music. He has made great steps to repair his image by releasing clean music about love, respect, and family. In an interview, Snoop said, "I have power and with that power comes great responsibility; so no longer will I use this gift to pull us down but lift us up." Now it's not all hip-hop's fault. We have to make better choices and conduct ourselves as responsible people. It also doesn't help to be fed false, one-sided information that makes all black youth feel unworthy of being saved, as though they deserve police brutality and other acts of unfair treatment. Nor do they need a soundtrack of their own self-destruction. I know it's hard, but we must start somewhere. Many of us have never even told our brothers that we love them. We have been made to believe that it's wrong for one man to tell another man that he loves him. Even the very thought of it makes most of us tense up, but we can call each other n%*!as and MFs all day, and we're fine with that. Unfortunately, we're learning this far too late in life. It wasn't until I engaged myself into manhood training class that I witnessed true brotherhood in action. I saw how easy it was to show genuine love and concern for one another at any given time. I remember one evening after class they were selling dinners, and Brother Mike and I sat down to eat and Brother Donnie was at the table as well. Brother Mike said to Brother Donnie, "Are you eating?" Brother Donnie said he only had car fare to get home. I watched Brother Mike share half of all he had with that brother, and it moved me. Later, I told Brother Mike how his kindness impressed me; it was then that he said to me, "Brother Derik, if you have a bowl of soup and your brother doesn't have any, half of your soup belongs to your brother." I have never forgotten that. There is so much power in the words we use toward each other as men; we have been beaten down so badly by the cold world that we don't even think we deserve to be loved. We've been held under by the pressure of life for so long that we have been emotionally drowned. Some of us come from homes filled with so much darkness that the only light we see is that emitting from the inner reflection of a brother saying, "I love you." Love your brother as yourself; it's the only way out of this dark pit of self-hatred.

I know it's hard, but we must start somewhere.

IMAGINATION

PUSH4

PROGRESS

Walt Disney: Today Disney rakes in billions from merchandise, movies and theme parks around the world, but Walt Disney himself had a bit of a rough start. He was fired by a newspaper editor because, "he lacked imagination and had no good ideas." After that, Disney started a number of businesses that didn't last too long and ended with bankruptcy and failure. He kept plugging along, however, and eventually found a recipe for success that worked.

Step Seven
Respect for women
❧ ✤ ❧

"If there were no god, the only thing worthy of worship would be the woman."
— **The Honorable Minister Louis Farrakhan**

This subject can utterly confirm or deny our place in manhood based on how we handle women. We must understand that if we ever want to be respected as men, then we must treat women with respect. Nations around the world judge men by the care and upkeep of their women, and if that's the case, than it's not looking too good for us. Our music, movies, and videos help to destroy the image of our women. Women are the second self of the creator and should be handled with the utmost respect and care. It's bad enough that we don't protect our sisters, but some of us who call ourselves men are even abusive to women. Listen, brothers, if you find yourself being abusive to a woman in any way—physical, mental, or verbal—I urge you to get help. As a young man, I learned early in life not to put my hands on a woman. I was raised with my two sisters and a beautiful mother, and I'd be deeply upset if someone were to abuse them in anyway. As I grew older, I was blessed enough to travel in a circle of men who made examples of men who took it upon themselves to abuse women. I truly believe that to correct a sick-minded individual who takes pride in such low actions, we must make examples of them. Some guys say, "But she hit me first," but I don't care. KEEP

YOUR HANDS TO YOURSELF. If you feel like you have to beat her, leave her. A woman should also keep her hands to herself as well; we are not each other's punching bags. So if you feel like you have to hit something, hit the books, hit the gym, but never a woman. NO REAL MAN HITS A WOMAN!

Develop your plan

"He, who fails to plan, plans to fail." —Proverb

A s we travel throughout the inner cities across America, we can find masses of young black males standing on the corners aimlessly. This leads to all levels of crime and imprisonment at alarming rates, and no sensible person wants this for themselves or their sons. This is in no way a coincidence. It's a clear sign that they're in real trouble. It's a fact that young black men have been gravely uneducated on the truth of our history; by no means am I saying we're not educated because we are. But we're not educated with the knowledge of ourselves. As a black man, I can't speak for all people, but it's a fact that if the self-love and respect that was tampered with isn't put back in place, we're a bomb waiting to implode. Notice I said "implode" and not "explode"; when self-hatred and the ignorance of self-knowledge continues to fester, it make one self-destructive. This is why on the TV you see the murder rate rising higher and higher due to black-on-black crime in our communities. Our behavior is a direct response to the rate of broken homes, lack of true love, and the high diet of ignorance that was consumed through our upbringings. Now I'm sure those of you with your PhD, doctorate degrees, and well-laid careers might want to jump down my throat right now, but I'm not talking to you. I'm talking to the young man standing in the alley with a package of illegal drugs on him who wanted more out of life but just couldn't put the pieces together. I'm talking to the young man who feels like the lyrics coming out of the radio are the blueprint and instructions for life. I'm talking to the young man at the end of a five-year prison sentence about to be released with no answers. Try to remember, it's not what happens to us, it's what we do afterwards. This is the part where you have to plug in and power up, brothers. The longest road to your dreams is the one that never starts. We have to apply the points and principles in order to bring our vision into fruition. Deep down inside, you know there's more out here for you and all you have to do is "set a fix" and lock in on it. Step-by-step you must keep adding to yourself; every time you read and study, you increase your potential to become great.

Step Nine
Get up, get out, and get something
✖ ❖ ✖

"A journey of a thousand miles begins with a single step."
—*Confucius*

It all starts with you—remember that. Whatever you want to be, whatever you want to do, wherever you want to go begins with you. Brothers, we cannot achieve our dreams by putting in half of the effort and awaiting the full reward. It's not wise to sleep most of the day away; awaking late in the day robs us of valuable time that could be used productively. Whenever I studied any of the people I admired, I noticed that they all had one thing in common: they all woke up between the hours of 3:30 a.m. and 6:00 a.m. to start their day. These men are multi-millionaires of Fortune 500 companies, yet they agree that the earlier you start the day, the more progress you make. Now I'm not saying you should jump up at 3:00 a.m.—that's up to you—but I do agree that you should start your day at the top. Now waking up early just to lay around watching DVDs and putting in hours on video games isn't wise either; you must move to obtain anything. Get out of the house; look up people, places, and things going on around you that have something to do with your goals and dreams. I remember as a young man starting out, I had to do something, so I surrounded myself with people who were productive, and they helped to guide me in the direction of all sorts of jobs. I did whatever I could to make an honest living for myself. You

41

name it, I have tried it, from flipping burgers to moving furniture, I did whatever I could to progress and stay out

> *It all starts with you - remember that.*

of trouble. It wasn't until I started applying myself that I began to focus on my goals and take the necessary steps to make them a reality. In order to focus on my goals, I had to make some changes and that meant less hanging out, fewer video games, and more studying and rest. I noticed that when I got up early, it was easier to be on time. I'd prepare most of what I needed the night before so I had an agenda set. Before I knew it, I was well on my way to making my dreams come true. So reach deep within yourself and get up, get out, and get something—you deserve it.

Step Ten
A positive attitude
ॐ ⚜ ॐ

"Nothing can stop the man with the right mental attitude from achieving his goal; nothing on earth can help the man with the wrong mental attitude."
—*Thomas Jefferson*

It's extremely important that you believe in yourself. I mean even if no one else rides for you, your ideas, and what you're passionate about, then you should. It will take every ounce of will and determination to stay focused when everyone around you lacks your enthusiasm. You must strive to keep a positive attitude in all you do; there will be days when you'll have to not only think, but know, the value of goals and dreams. In order to maintain a healthy winning attitude, you'll have to think, act, and move as if you have already won. Treat people with the greatest respect, be quick to share a kind word, and watch the vibe of positivity begin to surround you. Remember that everyone wants to feel important and noticed; it's human nature. Try to study and learn as much as you can about the daily habits of the successful people you admire and absorb key points to build you arsenal of positive energy. Now don't get me wrong, on this journey you will face hardship and trials that will absolutely floor you. However, these very events help to build and shape the zeal of a man. Remember that nothing worth having comes without difficulty attached to it, so you should look and prepare for the difficulties that come with achieving manhood. Some of us have gotten into trouble in the past and some of us are in trouble now, but you must understand that just because you might fall down, you don't have to stay down. Believe me, I'm not the smartest man, so I had to take time out to study that much harder to reach my goals. For those of us who find ourselves behind the eight ball with a bad record, this only means we'll have to push that much harder and study that much longer. See the obstacles as opportunities to push and apply yourself. Despite our shortcomings, we can still reach greatness. We can still do the very best we can to make things better than ever. Yes, the haters will come; they want to see you fall, so use them. Just as a car needs fuel, so do you; use your haters as fuel on your journey to success.

RESILIENCE

PUSH4

Henry Ford: While Ford is today known for his innovative assembly line and American-made cars, he wasn't an instant success. In fact, his early businesses failed and left him broke five times before he founded the successful Ford Motor Company.

PROGRESS

Step Eleven
Stand on your own two feet
❧ ✤ ❧

"Without a struggle, there can be no progress."
—Frederick Douglass

This is one of the most important topics we'll be addressing on this journey, brothers, and that's independence. I must admit that I'm highly disappointed in the overwhelming amount of young able-bodied men living at home with their parents. Let's be straight up, if you're returning from college, the military, or maybe you had the honor of helping to take care of an ill loved one—these are some of the legitimate reasons to still be living at home after the age of 25. I even hear men say, "I stay home because I'm trying to help them out!" Stop brothers. I've seen grown men in their mid-30s are talking this same foolishness, even moving their girl in the basement with them. First, we must understand that this only robs a man of the strength and experience needed to survive as a man. Every man should strive to maintain a place of his own—granted it will be tough and you might fall flat on your butt, but this will only make you stronger. Before we can care for and maintain a woman, we should first balance a room or apartment of our own. Some men refuse to do this, but they want a woman in their life. It takes responsibility and

You must strive to keep a positive attitude in all you do;

47

integrity to handle a woman. She needs to be maintained, and if you're not even maintaining the roof over your head, then it's not possible to properly care for a woman. There are some women out here who will accept a man with no job who lives at home; however, she'll see you as a child and rightfully so. Here is a hard-working woman out here maintaining herself, and here you are a big grown man in the basement at your mother's house. No, sir, step it up. So what if you have a brand new car, clothes, and other trinkets? You live at home like a child. Women want someone they can count on to have experience, someone who can shoulder the responsibilities of a family, and if you're living at home, then you're ducking your own growth and development. Get up and stand on your own two feet.

Step Twelve
Fatherhood
ᗧᗣ ✚ ᗣᗧ

"Nothing I've ever done has given me more joys and rewards than being a father to my children."
—*Bill Cosby*

Fatherhood is a very sensitive area for many young men for many reasons, ranging from abusive fathers to completely absent fathers. This depletes a great deal of drive out of a young man due to the natural inclination to the father. If you experience abandonment or abuse from that source, it creates a gaping hole of pain that can be carried well into adulthood. Sadly, 72% of black children are raised in a single parent home, and most are by single mothers. In many ways, this is part of the problem and the overwhelming number of misguided young black men in the streets and prisons. It's no coincidence that most of the young men who grow without a father or male role model in their lives end up embedded in drugs, crime, and gangs. I remember having a father in my home and all the benefits it entailed—order, care, guidance, and for the most part, a blueprint on how to conduct myself. I say this not to take anything away from my mother, who did an outstanding job, but even she knew she couldn't teach me how to be a man. I honor my mother with every fiber of my being for stepping aside unselfishly to allow her son a chance to receive what he needed. Brothers, most of our community has been gravely misled to believe that we are an "option" in the lives of our children and that we aren't an important figure in the home. In our community, many women have adopted a foolish mindset to seek a child support check rather than a father's presence in their children's lives. Now I'm not overlooking the percentage of men who refuse to take care of their children; they're wrong and it's not fair to that woman or that child. I can't stress how important it is for a man to help raise a child he helped to bring into this world. Brothers, please, I can't be more honest with you when I say I know it's difficult, especially when you are no longer in a relationship with the mother of your children. However, just because the two of you aren't together, your responsibility remains with the children. You must override the anger and stay focused. These types of situations can become so far out of hand. For instance, some men are very much on top of their relationship with their child yet the mother goes above and beyond to cause even greater problems. I remember what things were like after my father left, and even though I was 13 at the time, I really wished he could have stayed longer to give me more guidance. It changed everything, and even though we carried on, I felt that empty space differently than the rest of my family did. My children's mother never really knew her father and it played a horrible role in how she related to me. Now I've always said that I would never leave my children the way my father left me. I thought that she would feel the same way about our children because of her father's absence in her life. That couldn't have been further from the truth. As I write these

> *Actions speak louder than words, by God's grace.*

words, she and I have the worst relationship in my life. While that makes no sense at all, she's more than welcome to feel as she wishes. However, with the understanding of how important it is to be in my children's lives, I have never given up. I do anything and everything I can just to be with them—go to the school and go to the house, whatever. To this very date, she has tried harder than ever not only to stop my connection but also to destroy it. I truly love my children, and I would never hurt them; however, they have been fed lies to make them think I'm some kind of monster. I have had my driver's license suspended, have attended "deadbeat dad" classes, and even had my paychecks garnished do to errors in child support records. Despite what has been done and said, I strive to set an example for my children. Actions speak louder than words, by God's grace. I understand how unfair things can be, but we have to keep pushing and never stop. Now if you have a positive relationship with the mother of your children, that's wonderful, and do everything in your power to help her with the responsibilities and the children will develop into outstanding adults. Brothers, when it's your time to spend time with the children, do what you're supposed to do and spend time with them. Many women complain about the way men pick up the children only to drop them off elsewhere instead of spending the time with them. This behavior isn't wise at all; of course, sometimes things come up, but try to avoid such issues; stay focused and steady on the course to become a great father.

FOCUS

PUSH4

Michael Jordan: Most people wouldn't believe that a man often lauded as the best basketball player of all time was actually cut from his high school basketball team. Luckily, Jordan didn't let this setback stop him from playing the game and he has stated, "I have missed more than 9,000 shots in my career. I have lost almost 300 games. On 26 occasions I have been entrusted to take the game winning shot, and I missed. I have failed over and over and over again in my life. And that is why I succeed."

PROGRESS

Step Thirteen
Never give up
➤❧ ✤ ❧➤

"When the world says, 'Give up,' Hope whispers, 'Try it one more time.'" —Unknown

We must truly embrace and understand this step. Many of us have made decisions of which we aren't too proud; in fact, we might be downright ashamed of them. Well, brothers, the first step in dealing with this is to accept it, own it, and move on. We have to understand that life will always have difficulties; sometimes, our judgment under different circumstances won't be as clear. It takes time to gain a better understanding and that comes from living, so even though we may stumble, fall, or even fail, we can always get back up. Life can deal you a cold hand at times and it can make things very uncomfortable, but remember that the pain is temporary. The tough times that you face might be hard and they might feel unbearable, but as bad as it becomes, it will pass. We must learn to understand and accept the hard times in order to appreciate the good times. Those dark, cold rainy days help you to enjoy and embrace the warm rays of sunshine and clear blue skies. I remember when I was studying for the firefighter exam; I studied hours and hours and even went out and bought books. I did what I thought was the best that I could do to prepare for the exam. Finally, on the day of the test, I woke up extra early to dress and have a nice big breakfast. Then, I headed out. I arrived, and hundreds of people from all over the east coast had traveled to take this exam, but I was more than ready. Everyone scrambled for a seat as the staff began to pass out test booklets; the tension was so thick, you could cut it with a knife. An instructor looked at her watch and said, "You have three hours to complete this exam. Start now." I opened the test booklet and you would have thought it was written in Korean the way my jaw dropped. I couldn't seem to remember a thing. I was puzzled and I second-guessed myself with each answer. The three hours seemed to be slipping by so quick that before I knew it, I heard the instructor yell, "Times up! Turnover you booklets; as I made my way home, I felt unsure about the test but I kept thinking positively, anticipating that it went well. Days later, I checked the mail more than I ever have in my life, looking for my test results. Finally, the letter arrived and I placed it on the table and just stared at it for a while before opening it. I opened the letter only to find my greatest fear come true: "Unfortunately, you didn't meet the required score needed to continue…" I felt so low because I studied so hard, and I felt as though I let my family down as well as myself. In my mind, I blew my shot at a better life for myself, and I really had a hard time getting over that. After a few days went by and I started to feel better, and I understood that in order to move on, I'd have to get over this. I wasn't going to waste another day feeling down on myself, so I hit the books even harder this time. I really had to reach deep down inside to find the strength to fight for my dream.

No matter what happens, keep going and never give up.

I waited and took the exam again. Now I'd be lying if I said it wasn't difficult, but I kept going, and now by the grace of God and self-determination, I work with some of the country's best men and women in the Baltimore City Fire Department. All I'm saying is that you're going to experience losses, setbacks, and failures, but you must get back up, dust yourself off, and try again. Some of us have blemishes on our record due to poor choices we made in the past, but I'm here to tell you, brothers, that if you truly repent and honestly want to turn your life around, you can. No matter what happens, keep going and never give up.

PERSEVERANCE

PUSH4

Albert Einstein: Most of us take Einstein's name as synonymous with genius, but he didn't always show such promise. Einstein did not speak until he was four and did not read until he was seven, causing his teachers and parents to think he was mentally handicapped, slow and anti-social. Eventually, he was expelled from school and was refused admittance to the Zurich Polytechnic School. It might have taken him a bit longer, but most people would agree that he caught on pretty well in the end, winning the Nobel Prize and changing the face of modern physics.

PROGRESS

Step Fourteen
Overthrow your vices
ᗡᕼ ⚜ ᕼᗡ

"Chains of habit are too light to be felt until they are too heavy to be broken." —Warren Buffett

If we ever want to reach our true potential as men, we have to storm the castle of our vices and break free of the negative pull they have on our hearts and minds, regardless of the vice—drugs, prostitution, alcohol, gambling, pornography etc. If you believe you don't have any vices, dear brother, think again. Anything that holds you down or overpowers your mind, where you feel as though you must have it to function is a vice or addiction. Now some might think that because the vice of their choice isn't a drug it isn't harmful, but it can be just as destructive if not more. While some vices cause physical health problems, others cause the decay of moral fiber, forever altering your connection with your friends and family. Habits, such as gambling, can give you a winning rush of dominance and send you spiraling down an ever-growing pit of financial loss. Many have lost not only their money but also the money and property of the people around them who, out of love, tried to help and support them. Another issue for many men is pornography. This was an obstacle for me in my development process. It began harmlessly but grew into a bigger issue that seemed to sneak up on me, and it consumed a great deal of my focus. It illuminated emotions only needed in the company of a special woman and lessened the value of such a connection. I began building this unrealistic image of a woman and my connection to her because of porn. I had become desensitized mentally to the needs of a woman beyond the bedroom, and trust me brother, this is not where you want to be as a man. Luckily, I managed to catch myself before losing total control; I was able to overthrow my vices for porn and re-establish my focus. Now you watch whatever you wish, I'm just sharing what was an issue for me so that we have a clear understanding that too much of anything isn't good. I'm sure some men might be suffering from addictions deeper than what I encountered. I encourage anyone dealing with such issues to reach out and obtain help. Multiple outreach hotlines will be listed in the back of this book. I believe you can overpower any addiction you might be suffering from with the proper help.

Step Fifteen
Give yourself the gift of giving to others
꙰ ✿ ꙰

"Happiness doesn't result from what we get, but from what we give." —Dr. Ben Carson

The rigorous course a man travels while seeking self-improvement can take a lot out of him; sometimes, the last thing on our minds is giving even more of ourselves. Many people have nowhere else to turn, and this can be a chance to help someone else and an opportunity to enrich your life by assisting others in need. Nothing heals better than truly serving from your heart to help those less fortunate. I remember when I was experiencing a very trying time in my life, and I was stressed over what I thought were big problems. Then, I had a closer look at the homeless rate in my city. Unfortunately, that rate has reached record numbers in Baltimore, Maryland, at 4,088 and growing. Can you imagine being out in all kinds of weather conditions with nowhere to go, no means of income, and no place to call home other than some makeshift structure? The very thought of living under such conditions caused my heart to race with fear, so I began to educate myself on homelessness. After learning more about this problem, I began to look for ways to help. I went online and set up meetings to register as a volunteer feeding the homeless wherever they needed me. I've always had an image of what I thought homelessness looked like until I was given a chance to volunteer with Bea Gaddy's feed the Hungry program. When I went to the recreation center on Thanksgiving Day, all of my preconceived notions crumbled. I was brought face-to-face with all races, genders, ages, and cultures. As I made my way into the building, I could hear someone yelling my name from the crowd, "Hey Derik! Derik!" I turned to see who it was, and to my surprise, I saw my best friend Larry from elementary school squeezing through the crowd of people. I greeted him as I always have with the upmost respect. Larry looked out for me like a big brother even though we were the same age, and I loved him like a brother. He briefly shared with me his situation. I gave him my contact information and we promised to stay in touch. I helped Larry to his seating area then reported to my assigned post to begin serving in the food line. As the room started to fill, a tall gentleman came up to be served, and just as I went to ask what would he like, and a little

Nothing heals better than truly serving from your heart to help those less fortunate.

girl peeked from behind him and said, "Something to eat please." I smiled but inside I was crying like a child as I seated them and fixed their plates. You would've thought I was serving royalty the way I handled the people who walked through those doors, and I felt like a millionaire inside. All the stress I was feeling melted away that evening; serving didn't make my life perfect, but it did help me to be grateful for what I have. It didn't stop there. I went home and cried like a baby. I really wanted to wipe homelessness off the earth myself. I started signing up for volunteer work anywhere I could: Thanksgiving meals, stocking pantries, and giving out winter coats at the local firehouse, you name, it I did my best to help. Now I'm not saying that you need to run out and spend all of your days off at the local shelter. Do as you wish, but treat yourself to the gift of giving. It will change the way you see life. It's a whole world out there; there's enough for everyone to do their part. Always try to remember, "To whom much is given, much is required," so we should do our best to help those less fortunate than we are.

SUCCESS

PUSH4

Thomas Edison: In his early years, teachers told Edison he was "too stupid to learn anything." Work was no better, as he was fired from his first two jobs for not being productive enough. Even as an inventor, Edison made 1,000 unsuccessful attempts at inventing the light bulb. Of course, all those unsuccessful attempts finally resulted in the design that worked.

PROGRESS

Step Sixteen
How fast things can change!

"Some changes look negative on the surface, but you will soon realize that space is being created in your life for something new to emerge." —Eckhart Tolle

I can remember it like it was yesterday. I was walking down the tiers of B-block in the Maryland State Penitentiary, where hundreds of men are incarcerated. My job was to patrol, inspect, and account for each inmate housed in my area. The inmates' charges ranged from drug trafficking to murder, and everything in between; nonetheless, some carried on as if they had no worries at all. I often wondered what had triggered these men—sons, husbands, and fathers—to go off track; sometimes, I'd respectfully ask them. Even though I was on the opposite side of the inmate population, I had managed to acquire a solid level of respect from both officers and inmates throughout the prison system. Because of this mutual respect, the inmates were willing to communicate with me. Whenever I worked, I turned the entire wing into a think-tank, if you will. Although many topics were covered in our discussions, I strived to maintain a positive uplifting tone, and some even shared their own stories of trial and error. As time went on, discussion topics continued to surface, and the discussions were requested throughout the institution.

When given the opportunity to take the floor, in most discussions the men traced the rise of their ill behavior back to poor decisions made in haste. One of the stories in particular, shared by a young man named Paul, moved me. He told us about being the first in his family to finish high school and to attend college. He expressed how proud his family was of him and how happy he was with his life at the time. He showed us pictures of his high school graduation and his first year on the college campus with all his friends. After diligently completing another semester, he made plans to go home to see his family. It was a joy for his parents to have him back home, sharing stories and catching up. After the outstanding home-cooked meal his mom made, Paul headed out the door to see some of the guys he used to hang out with around the old neighborhood. As soon as he hit the block, "Ahh ... It's Joe College!" yelled one of his closest friends Warren, whom Paul had known since childhood. They laughed and talked about old times. Out of all the guys whom Paul hung out with, Warren was happy for Paul going off to school. He even paid for all his gear and helped with his books while he was away. Warren proudly told everybody how smart Paul was for leaving the streets behind even though he was deeply embedded in drugs and gang life himself. That didn't stop Paul from showing love whenever he saw him. A few days later, Warren had the guys plan a get-together for drinks at the local lounge; the place was jumping just like old times but something seemed to be bothering Warren.

"What's up Warren, you good?"

"Yeah; it's nothing. Let's walk."

As they walked, Warren lit up a cigarette shaking his head and said, "I think I really messed up this time P."

"What's really going on?" Paul asked.

"It's money issues," said Warren, "but I didn't take it. It was short when it got to me. I swear."

Just as they were talking, a truck pulled up and two dudes hopped out with a gun drawn. "Run P!" Warren yelled, as he rushed the guy with the gun the minute he got close enough.

Paul wanted to run, but he saw them struggling for the gun. Two shots went off as Paul rushed the guy. Warren slowly slid down the wall, clutching his chest as Paul wrestled the gun away, firing four shot into the dude as the other sped off in the truck. Paul quickly grabbed Warren in is arms, "Somebody help—somebody please!" With tears running down his face, Paul was in shock.

Warren pulled at his sweatshirt, gasping for breath. He pulled Paul closer, asking him over and over, "Did you—did—did you get the books I sent you, Joe College?"

"I got them man. Stay with me, Warren. Breathe man—come on!"

Lights and sirens closed in and surrounded the area as Paul sat holding his dying friend.

Paul was sentenced to twelve years for second-degree murder. His life, hard work, and progress in college were all shattered with the judge's sentencing. Paul's family was devastated as they watched their son escorted out of the courtroom in chains. Some things simply cannot be avoided; however, we must try our best to be aware of our surroundings at all times so that we don't become a victim of our environment.

DREAM

PUSH4

Harrison Ford: In his first film, Ford was told by the movie execs that he simply didn't have what it takes to be a star. Today, with numerous hits under his belt, iconic portrayals of characters like Han Solo and Indiana Jones, and a career that stretches decades, Ford can proudly show that he does, in fact, have what it takes.

PROGRESS

Step Seventeen
Nothing's just going to fall in your lap
❧ ✤ ❧

"Some people dream of success...while others wake up and work hard at it." —Unknown

Anything worth having comes with a price, and the sooner we understand this, the better off we'll be. No matter your path, if you desire to be successful, you will have to invest your time, energy, and focus. I know it sounds difficult, but consider the countless hours spent partying, chasing the ladies, or uploading to a Face book page. You will have to change the way you spend your time and hone in on what you want to accomplish. Remember, nobody owes you anything, and all of your hopes and dreams will only come into fruition through your effort. If you want more money, a nice home, your own business—whatever it might be, you must position your heart and mind in order to make it happen. So be ready to sweat and grind your way through all of the obstacles and challenges that might come up to deter you from your goals. It's important that you consider and document your thoughts, dreams, and goals, so that you can create the blueprint to your success. Desire feeds the will; there is nothing like good ole' wants and needs to fuel your drive for accomplishment.

If you find a wall of opposition in between you and everything you hope and dream of, you must go over, under, around, or through it if you want to reach the other side. No one will have to tell you to wake up earlier or stay up later; if it's everything to you, that one shot at opportunity, you'll fight hard to make it happen. I know this because I used to be the one who slept until noon and stayed up partying well into the morning. I was the guy who didn't read and study like I should've, knowing I had a quiz and test coming up. I got the D- grades and summer school classes because I did things the hard way. The moment I started to see that I was only going to get out of life what I put into it, my life took a complete turn. Once I felt more rested and relaxed after going to bed at a decent hour, no one had to tell me when to go to bed; after seeing that waking up earlier increased my chances of accomplishing more, nobody had to tell me when to wake up. It's that simple. If you really want or need something, you will align your time, priorities, and focus to achieve it. You will not sit and wait for it to fall in your lap—because it never will.

No matter your path, if you desire to be successful, you will have to invest your time, energy, and focus.

Step Eighteen
Choose your heroes wisely
❧ ✤ ❧

"The measure of choosing a good hero depends on your ability to find good in the hero you choose"
-Derik Barnes

Many young men were raised in broken or inadequate homes, and we suffered mostly due to the lack of decent role models and father figures. Because of this, many young men gravitate toward negative guidance rather than positive. While there aren't enough positive examples, we must be real with ourselves and understand that there are far more negative examples and influences that can snare us. Now we all know that no matter what is taught to us, the decision is solely ours. So for everything it's worth, dear brothers, if and when you choose your heroes, choose them wisely, and make sure you can see a future in the example being set. You should be able to track the footsteps of their progress and clearly see that they have learned from the mistakes made, regardless of how small or large. Be realistic. In other words, don't live or follow with your head in the clouds. I say this because a young man can easily drop everything to start a rap career simply because Lil' Wayne has reached mega success. He might be very successful at what he does, but outside of being extremely talented, he loves what he does, and he has placed it ahead of most things in his life at some point. So while you may admire him and desire the same avenue of progress, ask yourself do you love this and are you willing to pay the price for that level of success? In addition, never follow someone's example that robs you of your individuality or that influences you to do things that could cost you your freedom or life. In other words, everything isn't for everybody, so study your role models carefully and strive to find yourself within the scope of admiration you have for them.

ELEVATION

PUSH4

Akio Morita: You may not have heard of Morita but you've undoubtedly heard of his company, Sony. Sony's first product was a rice cooker that unfortunately didn't cook rice so much as burn it, selling less than 100 units. This first setback didn't stop Morita and his partners as they pushed forward to create a multi-billion dollar company.

PROGRESS

Step Nineteen
Let's do the math
❧ ✤ ❧

"I can see patterns in events, and behaviors; in mathematics, I follow slower" — *Jacqueline Carey*

People do many different things for many different reasons, and most of the time, it's because someone they look up to or admire has preceded them or turned them onto it. Now this works in both a positive and negative way, particularly in the case of a young man yearning to be led, yet lacking guidance. This may not be the case for every young man, but of course, "an idle mind is the devil's workshop." With all the negativity our youth are exposed to, it is very easy to be vacuumed into poor choices. We hear so many of our elders saying, "When I was young, I wasn't even thinking about having a child until I was grown enough to understand." Yes, while this may be true, let's also take a closer look and be fair. Never has there been a generation so surrounded with madness as this one. We are imbedded in a sex-crazed world where the car you drive, the music you listen to, and the food you eat are all driven by sex. A world where a woman's backside is paraded everywhere you turn, and you can hear the filthiest songs at any time of day. Now you take that and subtract the guidance from two loving parents and chaos is what you have. It's no wonder the teen pregnancy rate is off the charts. Some of our elders say, "These kids have lost their minds." With all this violence today, you're right, but again, let's be fair. I'm not making excuses. I'm just showing the whole picture. Anytime you have a young man with no positive father figure or male role model, it becomes very easy for him to be guided in the wrong direction. Many of our inner-city communities are overrun with drugs, gangs, and violence. A broken home is a part of life that many young men never recover from; it rips down the soul of a boy who is internally begging for help. So much so that when his father left him, he yearned for his love so badly that he turned his attention away for his mother, away from school, and away from the Creator's way. He opened himself up to the streets. Now let's do some math. Take those circumstances and subtract the after-school programs, recreation centers, mentorship programs, and libraries. Now add tens of thousands of illegal guns, tons of illegal drugs, and build more prisons, and there you have it—madness. The same dangerous energy can be redirected and applied in a positive way if we approach the situation in another manner. First, those young men aren't out of control; *our* young men are out of control and need *our* help. Don't think for one moment that I don't support the youth who have overcome some of these dark horrifying conditions because I do, and I love them for doing so. However, for every one young man that has managed to escape this web of stagnation, there are five or ten more that remain tangled up in the system, in the streets—in the madness. There's a better way, and I want to be a link in the chain of greats who are working diligently to bring it about.

Step Twenty
Get out of your own way
❧ ✤ ❧

"What is the difference between a living thing and a dead thing? In the medical world, a clinical definition of death is a body that does not change. Change is life. Stagnation is death. If you don't change, you die. It's that simple. It's that scary." — Leonard Sweet

As time goes on and you begin to focus, you learn that life will throw some curve balls, some you'll never see coming. This causes us to have to stay one step ahead in order to stay focused. Now as hard as things can be and with all the opposition you may have to deal with, let's not make it any harder on ourselves. I'm sure we all like to chill with the guys, maybe even grab a cold one now and then. Remember your plan: if you want to progress as much as you say you do, then you'll be watchful. Let go of things that could potentially uproot your plans, such as marijuana or any drug. It makes no sense to make all these outer changes but to refuse to change within. I have to keep it real with you, brother, if you're still blazing up with your guys, you're sure to lock yourself out of the bigger picture. You cannot be serious about achieving your goals when you can't even piss clean. I have to be real, no decent job will ever hire you with such issues. It's less than intelligent to sabotage yourself and your chances like this. I know a young man trying to land a better job; he had a wife and kids who were counting on him as a husband and father. It was a long hard application process, which he completed, but when the time came to show and prove, his urinalysis was positive for marijuana. Two kids and a wife, and he blew an awesome opportunity. Even the burger joints are starting to crack down on this. If you want to do better, here's your chance. Don't let something so petty and weak hold you down; kick that and any other foolishness to the side. Get out of your own way, man, for real.

Step Twenty-One
Education
❧ ✦ ❧

"Education is the most powerful weapon, which you can use to change the world." — *Nelson Mandela*

I really cannot stress to you how important it is to get an education, even if it seems to be a real bore or burden. Your level of education will play a very important role in everything you do throughout your life. I have to be honest, I had no idea just how much my effort in education would play a part in my life. Brothers, in order to obtain a job or career that allows you to take care of yourself or your family properly, you will need a sound education. Things are completely different today, and every avenue of progress will require a degree or some level of training. Now when I speak of educating yourself, I'm not only referring to college. Education could be studying the specific field in which you're striving to embark on a career. Many young men find their true talent and skills by joining the military, and this too has its advantages. The military offers young men a chance to travel and see the world, earn funding for school, and master a skill that can go wherever they go. Unfortunately, a percentage of young males within the

> *Your level of education will play a very important role in everything you do throughout your life.*

inner cities require an environment more disciplined than most people, and the military offers just that, along with opportunities I mentioned. I have family members who have outstanding careers in the military, and they have made remarkable growth and progress. Many people may disagree with me for mentioning the armed services as an option, but when you've been to as many wakes and funerals for young men as I have, you won't only see it as an opportunity, but a life-saving decision. You should also remember that it's never too late to get an education, be it a G.E.D or a college degree. Some of the very people I admire the most had a late start for whatever reason, but they didn't let that stop them. They would always tell me that if they knew then what they know now, they would have taken school more seriously much sooner. All that I'm trying to convey to you, brothers, is that life can be far more difficult without an education than it is with an education. Give yourself the gift of a foundation on which you can build a brighter future.

Step Twenty-Two
The trap
❧ ✤ ❧

"Emancipate yourselves from mental slavery, none but ourselves can free minds." —Bob Marley

Trap: 1) a machination used for catching game or other animals; a mechanical device that springs shut suddenly 2) Any device, stratagem, trick, or the like for catching a person unaware.

Many times the drug game has been referred to as the "trap." We hear it in hip-hop songs and see it in the videos where people constantly brag about being in the "trap." Knowing just what a trap is, we must take a deeper look into the mindset of the individuals inside it. At one time or another, we've all had something or someone that we valued in our lives, and we did all we could to keep them safe and out of harm's way. Yet some of us place ourselves in situations that often cost us our freedom or our lives. Let's be honest and really pay close attention to how particular we are about our style of dress and keeping up with what everyone else has. Now some might say, "Wow, Derik, what in the world does this have to do with the trap?" Stay with me, and I'll show you.

Act I: Bait
This is how it all starts, watching countless hours of "tel-lie-vision" without proper debriefing to all the madness we're soaking into our minds. Our young men

are constantly fed this illusion of fast money and fame without educating themselves about the struggle, focus and sacrifices made to obtain such a lifestyle. Now I remember how bad I wanted some of those very items and would have done almost anything to get them, but fortunately, someone intervened with some real words of reason for me or my life might have fallen dangerously off course. Nowadays our young men might not be so lucky. Let's keep it real, some of our own brothers in the rap game are literally guiding our young men into the drugs and violent behavior. "Aw man, Brother Derik, I can't believe you said that!" Why not? It's the truth, I understand hip-hop and the artistic way of telling your story about the come up, but when it's your tenth and fifteenth album and your still "trap'n" as they say wow man, what are you trying to inspire in our young men?" I don't have to call no names; they know who they are. For a young man without guidance, this builds a blueprint of destruction in his heart and mind.

Next, surround them with drug-infested communities that seem to provide the answer to the desire for this instant lifestyle they saw on the "tell-lie-vision." Oh and make sure that some of the countless liquor stores in the community bear the images of some of the biggest artist endorsing alcohol, which is one of the number one killers of the community. Don't forget to soak the radio airwaves with lyrics of senseless violence and disrespect for women. Then, make sure some of the world's most dangerous guns find their way into the community. Are you getting the feeling that a trap is being set?

Act II: Trap

Hotel owners strive to keep the occupancy percentage as high as possible in order to be deemed successful, and the same goes for prisons. There are 1,700 hundred prisons all across the country at both the state and federal level. They don't build these intuitions to keep them empty, and we would be fools to think that. Now how do you keep a prison full? Well, other than your average violators, you may have to bait the hook a bit, and this is where it becomes more strategic. Surely sound-minded, focused young men aren't walking into the prisons by the hundreds and saying, "Here I am, I'm ready to throw my life away." In the prison system, a revolving door continues to turn with repeat offenders. Statistics show that this door continues until individuals are finally hit with a serious charge that causes them to do more time in the prison system. While working as a correctional officer in Maryland's institutions, almost every inmate I encountered had been in and out of some form of institution as a teen. It's clear that the poor and low-income communities are targeted to fuel the institutional beast known as the prison system. So take a moment and think about it: you risk your life and freedom for a drop in the bucket that ultimately drowns you and hundreds of thousands like you. We have to be wise today, brothers. Study the hunters in the wild and how they place their traps in specific locations. Some

All the things you could ever want and need will all be granted to you through hard work, patience, and sacrifice.

even camouflage themselves to blend in so that they can surround their prey. The targeted prey walks into the area unaware that it's totally surrounded and in the scope of the hunter's crosshairs. Notice how the hunter is careful not to make a sound that could startle the prey, so he's very quiet. In the hood, absolute silence is needed. They can't know we flooded the community with liquor stores, drugs, and guns (traps). Just like the prey that's unaware that he's surrounded, we too walk the streets unaware of our surroundings. Look around, man, this isn't a game! You have to open your mind and watch what you put in it. If it wasn't a trap, why do so many young men often meet the same fate as their fathers, uncles, brothers, and friends? It's foolish to be in the trap and not make others aware of the trap you have fallen into. You never see animals in the wild returning to the trap after escaping, and if they were caught in a trap, they would never fail to warn the others of such harm. You must understand that you are the prey, you are the one within the crosshairs of society, and you're trapped! As young men, we laugh, dance, and sing while we're being swallowed completely by this beast of a system. We repeat the very same foolish steps as those before us. As a survivor of the dark, trapped mindset, I'm sounding the alarm: "It's a trap, go back to school, stop sitting in front of that TV all day! It's a trap!" Try to stay focused and do your best not to be fooled into believing that this self-destructive lifestyle is the only way out, brother. All the things you could ever want and need will all be granted to you through hard work, patience, and sacrifice.

PERSISTENCE

PUSH4

Theodor Seuss Geisel: Today nearly every child has read *The Cat in the Hat* or *Green Eggs and Ham*, yet 27 different publishers rejected Dr. Seuss's first book *To Think That I Saw It on Mulberry Street.*

PROGRESS

Step Twenty-Three

See the world and expand yourself
❧ ✿ ❧

"The World is a book, and those who do not travel, read only one page." —St. Augustine

I remember sitting on the hill with my friends as a child watching the trains go by. I would always wonder where they were going. Do you ever wonder what it's like in other parts of the world? How they live? What they eat? You can look at pictures and search the internet until you're blue in the face, but the only way to feel the experience is to visit for yourself. I've heard so much about Mexico—the food and the people—but it wasn't until we traveled to see it for ourselves that I could experience its enriched culture. We visited many of the authentic Mexican restaurants and tasted some of the best food we've ever had. While on a tour of the sites, we were blessed to see the Mayan Temples, which were simply amazing. My wife and I were embedded in hospitality and soaked in kindness our entire visit, and we'll always remember the beautiful people of Mexico. After such an outstanding experience, our desire to see more of the world would take us to the Island of Jamaica. All my life I've felt a direct connection to my brothers and sisters from the Caribbean. Growing up, my mother would play music by the great Bob Marley and the Wailers in the house. He had songs like "Get Up, Stand Up" and "Redemption Song" that seemed to move my soul even as a young boy. As my lovely wife and I arrived in Jamaica, sharing the same excitement, we were both mesmerized by the beautiful sites and by the people who greeted us. The resort we stayed at was incredibly beautiful and it felt as if we were returning home after a long journey the way they welcomed us with such love. After a few days on the resort, we arranged a ride into town to see more of our Jamaican family. The island and the people were even more beautiful as we went deeper into town. We shopped in many of the nice stores throughout the area, meeting people at every stop. Even though we were ignorant to the way things worked there, they were patient with us and our family never once took advantage of us. Our guide took us to eat in one of the town's best authentic Jamaican restaurants, and my wife and I had the best meal we have ever eaten. We then went up into the mountains and met with our Rastafarian family by the name of "Proff." He welcomed us into his home and shared with us many, many things that we promised never to repeat. However, I will tell you about the overwhelming love and pride the people have for the great Bob Marley, which seemed to emit from the hearts of everyone we met. Bob Marley vibrations of love and peace are felt around the world, striking the hearts of millions and millions to come, and we'll forever be thankful for such a blessing. So, brothers, understand that the whole world belongs to you—go see it!

OPPORTUNITY

PUSH4

Colonel Sanders: At 65 years old, after receiving a social security check for some 100 dollars, Mr. Sanders thought he should show the world he's not to be taken for granted. He could have chosen a different path, but decided to fight for his project. The project in case – his chicken recipe. His target group? Restaurants that would make his chicken, gain customers and sales and offer him a decent profit. Number of rejections? Over a 1000 in the whole country. He got one shot once. All that followed is history and legend and some damn fine chicken meals.

PROGRESS

Step Twenty-Four
How to deal with law enforcement
~~~ ✦ ~~~

"The corruption of the best things gives rise to the worst."
-David Hume

Sadly, I could fill the remaining pages with the names of our young men whom have lost their lives by way of law enforcement. Now while there are police officers who do an outstanding job protecting our communities; there is a percentage of them who unjustly abuse their authority. It's not our job as citizens to try and figure out who's the good cop and who's the bad cop. As law enforcement officers, they are sworn in under an oath to serve and protect the public. In the police academy they submit themselves to rigorous levels of training such as the proper use of force, constitutional/state laws/ civil rights and local ordinances. Unfortunately, character and integrity are traits that cannot be given out with a badge. It saddens me to say that in every city and state across this country there are some officers that patrol the streets with a heart and mind full of darkness. Unfortunately for us our children must travel these very same streets coming in direct contact with a beast in uniform. We have all heard it one too many times before, "I thought he had a gun" and because of this many young men and woman have lost their lives. Some of our young men are found hand cuffed and beaten to death by the police. It doesn't take much for things to escalate and get out of hand when dealing with an officer who feels that he is the law. Under these ugly conditions you must exercise a higher level of awareness.

I cannot address this issue without exposing how some of our young men, in particular, make it easy for them to abuse and gun us down in the streets. We fill the streets all hours of the night in droves, pants around our ankles with a pocket full of narcotics. Some of you have terrorized the neighborhood so bad that your elders no longer feel safe around you. Just think, who do you think "STOP & FRISK" is for? We have turned in on ourselves and for this you are looked at as "THE PROBLEM" by law enforcement everywhere. This isn't a game, they will kill you out here and there won't be an outcry for you. Our babies have to play in these blocks of death that you have created. Children 4 and 7 year olds being shot down like dogs all because you're in a shootout. You must stop the senseless killing of yourselves before we can ever expect anyone else too. I'm fully aware that this isn't all of our beautiful young men. Some of you are students, fathers, husbands that have nothing to do with this madness, yet you too may come into contact with corrupt cops.

If you are approached by law enforcement:

Stay calm; keep your hands visible at all times.
If asked to present your photo identification grant them that request (must have ID on your person at all times at age 18 and older).
You can request the officer's name and badge number and write them down.

If you're pulled over by the police:

Whenever you are pulled over by the police remember to remain calm. Keep in mind that the officer(s) are already in a heighten state of mind from the beginning. It isn't wise to start digging & searching the glove box prior to the officer approaching the vehicle. From the rear window all they see is movement or you a suspect reaching for a weapon. When you are able to safely pull over do so, following these key points can de-escalate the tension:

- If you have the music playing cut it off, this implies that you're paying attention.
- Place your hands on the stirring wheel, this way no objects can be confused for a weapon.
- Let the officer do the talking or questioning, this shows a level of respect for authority.
- Have your paperwork and driver's license available in event you need to display it.

If you wisely choose to remain silent at least until you have a chance to consult a lawyer, you should tell that to the officer.

- I want to talk to an attorney.
- I won't say anything until I talk to an attorney.
- I don't have anything to say.
- I don't want to talk to you.
- I claim my Miranda rights.

If they ask to search your person:

- Don't resist the search
- Tell them "You don't have permission but I will not stop you physically."
- Don't resist physically, say it verbally and do not use profanity.

If you are arrested:

- Don't resist
- You have the right to know the charges
- You can make two phone calls (family and lawyer)

Thank you

I want to thank everyone for supporting "The science of manhood" steps to self-improvement. For everyone who has opened their minds and ears to hear what I had to say. To the woman who has helped to encourage the males in their lives by way of the book, I thank you. I want to thank all of the bookstores and cafes' for your support. All the media host for having me as your guest or even mentioning the book. Thank you all from the bottom of my heart.

"Life is one big road with lots of signs. So when you're riding through the ruts, don't complicate your mind. Flee from hate, mischief, and jealousy. Don't bury your thoughts. Put your vision to reality. Wake up and live"!

-Bob Marley

References for Outreach

Domestic Violence

National Domestic Violence Hotline: 800-799-SAFE /800-799-7233 and 800-787-3224 (TTY). This hotline provides crisis intervention and referrals to local services and shelters for victims of partner or spousal abuse; English and Spanish speaking advocates are available 24 hours a day, seven days a week.

Crisis Intervention/Suicide

Boys Town Suicide and Crisis Line: 800-448-3000 or 800-448-1833 (TDD). This hotline provides short-term crisis intervention, counseling, and referrals to local community resources. Counsels on parent-child conflicts, marital and family issues, suicide, pregnancy, runaway youth, physical and sexual abuse, and other issues. It operates 24 hours a day, seven days a week for anyone in need.

National Drug Abuse Helpline

866-358-5270

Youth Crisis

National Youth Crisis Hotline: 800-448-4663. This hotline provides counseling and referrals to local drug treatment centers, shelters, and counseling services; it responds to youth dealing with pregnancy, molestation, suicide, and child abuse; it operates 24 hours a day, seven days a week.

National Runaway Safe line
800-786-2929

Drug-free world
The Foundation for a Drug-Free World is a nonprofit public benefit corporation that empowers youth and adults with factual information about drugs so they can make informed decisions and live drug-free. Drugfreeworld. org. From within USA: 888-NO-DRUGS (888-668-6378). To call from outside USA: +1-818-952-5260.

About the Author

The author hopes that this book will lead to serious investigation of this subject, with the aim of restoring and implementing the true Science of Manhood.

Derik Barnes was born and raised in the inner city of Baltimore, Maryland. He can be described as ambitious, focused, and intellectual—a go-getter. Despite early  exposure to the struggle for balance that all young men face, Derik overcame. Through struggle in his personal life, he felt it his responsibility to assume the position of "man of the house" at an early age. It was not always an easy task to choose the right path when so many of his friends chose another direction, but he continued on, knowing it would somehow pay off in the end. After graduating from high school, he became active in both the prison reform programs and community cleanup to help restore some of the very inner city streets he often traveled. Much like most of the city, those areas were no "walk in the park" and were considered some of the most crime and drug infested.

Derik's strong sense of personal security later landed him a career as a Maryland State Correctional Officer. During his eight years of employment as a corrections officer, he was required to secure various institutions throughout the state. With the respect and trust gained by those around him, including his colleagues and the inmates, Derik became very familiar with the patterns of the young men entangled in the prison system. As his desire to help others grew, Derik increased his efforts and later moved on to become a Baltimore city firefighter. By no means did this desired career move come easy, but it proved to be most rewarding. Moving about the city streets once again at a different capacity gave Derik a unique perspective on the issues concerning young men.

With this book, The Science of Manhood, Derik hopes to reach and inspire young men by sharing life experiences and strategies not only to revitalize these young men, but also to help generations of men to come.

CLEAR VISION

"Focusing on a brighter tomorrow."

Derik Barnes (President)

Email: (derikbarnesclearvision@gmail.com)

Notes

The Science of Manhood

Notes

The Science of Manhood